pearls of wisdom

For the Graduate Starting College

Shirley Perich

Grand Rapids, MI 49501

Pearls of Wisdom: For the Graduate Starting College

© 2002 by Shirley Perich

Published by Kregel Publications, a division of Krege
Inc., P.O. Box 2607, Grand Rapids, MI 49501. For mor
information about Kregel Publications, visit our We
site: www.kregel.com.

ISBN 0-8254-3559-5

Printed in the United States of America

2 3 / 06 05 04 03

pearls

of wisdom

No, dear friends,
I am still not all I
should be, but
I am focusing all
my energies on
this one thing:
Forgetting the past
and looking
forward to what
lies ahead.

Don't skip anything—
classes, homework,
meals, sleep...

....or a good party.
Have lots of fun.

I came
to give life—
life in all its
fullness.

John 10:10
(NCV)

You're gonna have
lab partners, study groups,
roommates, classmates,
hall mates...most likely
you'll even be
sharing a bathroom.

Sometimes you'll need
to be alone.

After he had sent them away, he went by himself up into the hills to pray. It was late, and Jesus was there alone.

Matthew 14:23
(NCV)

Sharing a living space the size of a large closet with another human being may present challenges now and again.

They don't mention it in the admissions packet, but this, too, is all part of your education.

Do to others
what you
would want them
to do to you.

Luke 6:31
(NCV)

You certainly can hang out with the yahoo who talks the loudest, argues the most, drinks the heaviest, and swears to make just about any point.

Spend time with the wise and you will become wise, but the friends of fools will suffer.

Proverbs 13:20
(NCV)

Don't cheat.
Your professor
isn't the only one
watching.

Doing right brings freedom to honest people, but those who are not trustworthy will be caught by their own desires.

Proverbs 11:6
(NCV)

Dorm food may not be the best. But, hey, you didn't have to go to the grocery store, chop vegetables, boil pasta, peel potatoes, or wash dishes.

Is it tasting any better?

I have learned the secret of being content in any and every situation, whether well fed or hungry, whether living in plenty or in want.

No one is going to hound you about, wake you up for, or drive you to church.

No sirree. You're on your own.

And let us not neglect our meeting together, as some people do.

Hebrews 10:25
(NLT)

What's your major?

You don't have
to answer that
question right away.
And guess what?
You can even
change your mind.

Just try to avoid
doing that your
senior year.

For this God is
our God for ever
and ever; he will
be our guide even
to the end.

Psalm 48:14
(NIV)

You may not have more than a few extra bucks of your own, but helping someone out with a little pizza or gas money is always a good thing.

Do not forget to
do good to others, and
share with them,
because such sacrifices
please God.

Hebrews 13:16
(NCV)

If this thought ever remotely crosses your mind—"Mom and Dad weren't really as out of it as I thought they were" (or any paraphrased version of this general concept)— write 'em a note and tell 'em.

Make your
father and mother
happy; give your
mother a reason
to be glad.

Proverbs 23:25
(NCV)

Chuggin' beer can
look like lots of fun.

Hearing you acted like
a goofball in front of
fifty people isn't.

Wine and beer
make people loud
and uncontrolled;
it is not wise
to get drunk
on them.

Proverbs 20:1
(NCV)

When you're feeling over-
whelmed (and you will)
what do you do?

Some people party.

Some people party
really hard.

Some people fidget.

Some people drop out.

Some people don't sleep.

And some people pray.

Do not worry about anything, but pray and ask God for everything you need, always giving thanks. And God's peace, which is so great we cannot understand it, will keep your hearts and minds in Christ Jesus.

Philippians 4:6–7
(NCV)

You'll run into people who'll let you know how wealthy their families are, how good their grades are, how magnificent their athleticism is, how cultured their travels have made them.

Don't reciprocate with tales of your own magnificence. (You'll be way more impressive.)

Respecting the LORD
and not being proud
will bring you wealth,
honor, and life.

Proverbs 22:4
(NCV)

Say your prayers.

LORD,
every morning
you hear my voice.
Every morning,
I tell you what
I need, and
I wait for your
answer.

Psalm 5:3
(NCV)

Your family may
be eating macaroni
and cheese to help
put you through your
chosen institution
of higher learning.

Don't be too shy
to say thanks.

The right word
spoken at the right
time is as beautiful
as gold apples in
a silver bowl.

Proverbs 25:11
(NCV)

Don't let all-nighters
become a way of life.

The LORD gives
sleep to those
he loves.

Psalm 127:2
(NCV)

You and your roommate
may find yourselves on
different schedules.

Be considerate or
the next nine months may
be the longest ones
of your life.

If you loudly greet
your neighbor early in
the morning, he will
think of it as a curse.

Proverbs 27:14
(NCV)

Eat candy bars
and milk shakes
in moderation.

Unless it's finals week.

It is not good
to eat too
much honey.

Proverbs 25:27
(NCV)

Study hard.

And in every work
that he began . . .
he did it with all
his heart. So he
prospered.

2 Chronicles 31:21
(NKJV)

Trashy music is not an art form no matter whose dorm room it's blasting out of.

My child,
hold on to wisdom
and good sense.
Don't let them out
of your sight.

Proverbs 3:21
(NCV)

Kindergarten or college. The rules don't change much: Be nice and tell the truth.

Don't ever forget
kindness and truth.
Wear them like a
necklace. Write them
on your heart as if on
a tablet.

Proverbs 3:3
(NCV)

Promiscuity is
hazardous to your
self-esteem.

When people are tempted and still continue strong, they should be happy. After they have proved their faith, God will reward them with life forever. God promised this to all those who love him.

James 1:12
(NCV)

Don't compare
yourself to
anybody else.

Each person has his own gift from God. One has one gift, another has another gift.

I Corinthians 7:7
(NCV)

Day planners
are a good thing.
Just be sure to
use a pencil.

People can make all kinds of plans, but only the LORD's plan will happen.

Proverbs 19:21
(NCV)

In the most
unlikely of places,
with the most
unlikely of persons,
you just may find
a friend.

Live in peace
with each other.
Do not be proud,
but make friends with
those who seem
unimportant.
Do not think how
smart you are.

Romans 12:16
(NCV)

Phone calls home.

Staying up late with your roommate.

Dinners in the cafeteria.

Study groups.

Parties.

Class debates . . .

Let your
conversation
be always
full of grace.

Colossians 4:6
(NIV)

Don't leave your dirty underwear or smelly socks lying around.

It's bad form.

Do all you can to live a peaceful life. Take care of your own business, and do your own work as we have already told you.

1 Thessalonians 4:11
(NCV)

If by chance your roommate leaves dirty underwear or smelly socks lying around, don't get too bent out of shape.

People without good
sense find fault
with their neighbors,
but those with
understanding
keep quiet.

Proverbs 11:12
(NCV)

After a few months
of rubbing elbows with
all those academicians,
resist the temptation
to feel like you've been
transformed into a true
intellectual possessing
a superior understanding of
the universe and all
its workings.

You'll be so much
easier to be around.

Fools do not want
to understand
anything. They only
want to tell others
what they think.

Proverbs 18:2
(NCV)

People will enjoy
giving you advice.
Put your thinking
cap on before you
follow any of it.

Fools will believe
anything, but the wise
think about what
they do.

Proverbs 14:15
(NCV)

Best grades
Good job
Great car
Cool clothes

Nothing wrong
with any of them.
Just keep your
priorities straight
in the process of
obtaining them.

Your heart will
be where your
treasure is.

Luke 12:34
(NCV)

The foundations for
lifetime friendships
are often begun
in college.

Some friends may ruin you, but a real friend will be more loyal than a brother.

Proverbs 18:24
(NCV)

Tired as you may be.
Hard as it is.
Don't be crabby.

Pleasant words are like
a honeycomb, making
people happy and
healthy.

Proverbs 16:24
(NCV)

Clean the bathroom when it's your turn.

Do everything
without complaining
or arguing.

Philippians 2:14
(NCV)

Aim high.

You will enjoy what you work for, and you will be blessed with good things.

Psalm 128:2
(NCV)

College is fun but, hey, it's
not always a bowl
of cherries, either.

God, you are my comfort when I am very sad and when I am afraid.

Jeremiah 8:18
(NCV)

Intelligence can
explain the theory
of quantum physics.

Wisdom is in awe
of its Author.

In him all the
treasures of
wisdom and
knowledge are
safely kept.

Colossians 2:3
(NCV)

Don't pay for anything
with quarters.

You'll need 'em
for laundry.

There is a time
for everything,
and a season for
every activity
under heaven.

Ecclesiastes 3:1
(NIV)

Esoteric matters
may be debated with
regular frequency...
involve yourself
cautiously.

Stay away from foolish and stupid arguments, because you know they grow into quarrels.

2 Timothy 2:23
(NCV)

Graduating magna cum laude from Harvard ain't half bad, but that isn't the only credential you need to "make it."

You can get the
horses ready for
battle, but it is the
LORD who gives
the victory.

Proverbs 21:31
(NCV)

Counselors can suggest courses of study. You can read books on all the different career choices. Hey, your parents may even have an idea or two regarding your future.

But it belongs to none of them.

The LORD himself
will go before you.
He will be with
you; he will not leave
you or forget you.
Don't be afraid and
don't worry.

Deuteronomy 31:8
(NCV)

You have an earthly family and a heavenly Father who love you and want these next four years to be a blast.

Work hard and play when you've earned it.

May he give you the
desire of your heart
and make all your
plans succeed. We will
shout for joy when
you are victorious
and will lift up our
banners in the name
of our God. May the
LORD grant all
your requests.

Psalm 20:4–5
(NIV)

My Own Pearls of Wisdom

My Own Pearls of Wisdom

_____
_____
_____
_____
_____
_____
_____
_____
_____
_____
_____
_____
_____
_____
_____
_____
_____
_____
_____
_____
_____

My Own Pearls of Wisdom

My Own Pearls of Wisdom

_____

_____

_____

_____

_____

_____

_____

_____

_____

_____

_____

_____

_____

_____

_____

_____

_____

_____

_____

_____

_____

My Own Pearls of Wisdom

My Own Pearls of Wisdom